Uniquely
Utah

Bianca Dumas and D. J. Ross

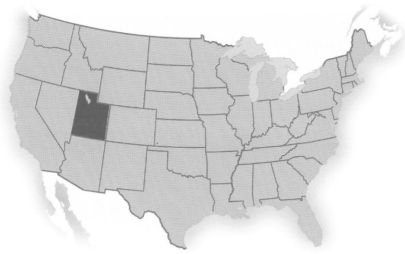

Heinemann Library
Chicago, Illinois

© 2004 Heinemann Library
a division of Reed Elsevier Inc.
Chicago, Illinois

Customer Service 888-454-2279

Visit our website at www.heinemannlibrary.com

Designed by Heinemann Library
Printed in China by WKT Company Limited.

08 07 06 05 04
10 9 8 7 6 5 4 3 2 1

**Library of Congress
Cataloging-in-Publication Data**

Dumas, Bianca.
   Uniquely Utah / Bianca Dumas.
      v. cm.—(State studies uniquely)
Includes bibliographical references and index.
Contents: Uniquely Utah—Utah's climate and
weather—Famous firsts—Utah state symbols—
Utah's history and people—Temple Square—Utah's
state government—Utah's culture—Utah's food—
Utah folklore and legends—Sports—Business and
products—Attractions and landmarks—Map of
Utah.
   ISBN 1-4034-4663-6 (library binding-
hardcover)—ISBN 1-4034-4732-2 (pbk.)
   1. Utah—Juvenile literature. [1. Utah.]
I. Title. II. Heinemann state studies.
   F826.3.D86 2004
   979.2—dc22
                              200025449

Acknowledgments
Development and photo research by
BOOK BUILDERS LLC

The author and publishers are grateful to the
following for permission to reproduce copyrighted
material:

Cover photographs by (top, L-R): Courtesy of Utah
Division of Travel Development, Utah Travel
Council, Utah Office of Tourism, Utah Office of
Tourism

Title page (L-R): Courtesy of Utah Travel Council,
Bud Freund/Alamy Images, Courtesy Utah Travel
Council; p. 5 Andre Jenny/Alamy Images; pp. 6, 7,
10, 11T, 12T, 14T, 14B, 25, 26, 30, 31, 39, 41, 42,
43 Courtesy of Utah Travel Council; p. 8, 12B, 20,
21 Courtesy of Utah Historical Society; p. 11B
Courtesy of Utah Division of Travel Development;
p. 15T Doug Wilson/Alamy Images; p. 15B Tom
Myers/Alamy Images; p. 16T D. Robert Franz/
Alamy Images; p. 16B Ed Young/Alamy Images;
p; 17T Geoff du Feu/Alamy Images; p. 17B
Carolina Biological Supply Company; p. 19 Tom
Till/Alamy Images; p. 24B Hulton Archive; pp. 27
Bud Freund/Alamy Images; p. 28 Courtesy of the
Utah Governor's Office; p. 33, 44 Alamy Images;
pp. 34 R. Capozzelli/Heinemann Library; p. 35
Julian Deghy/Alamy Images; p. 36, 37 Courtesy of
Utah Sports Information; p. 40 Walter
Bibikow/Alamy Images

Special thanks to Patricia Smith-Mansfield of the
Division of State History, Utah State Historical
Society for her comments in the preparation of
this book.

Every effort has been made to contact copyright
holders of any material reproduced in this book.
Any omissions will be rectified in subsequent
printings if notice is given to the publisher.

Cover Pictures

Top (left to right) Utah state flag, skier in
snow-capped mountains, Salt Lake City,
Mormon Church **Main** Rainbow Bridge

Some words are shown in bold, **like this.**
You can find out what they mean by looking
in the glossary.

Contents

Uniquely Utah

Unique means one of a kind. Utah is unique in many ways. It is the home of the Church of Jesus Christ of Latter-day Saints, or **Mormon** Church. It is also the location of Promontory Point, the site where the nation's first **transcontinental** railroads joined in 1869. Utah is a large state with only a few big cities. Within Utah's 84,990 square miles of land would fit the states of Maine, Vermont, New Hampshire, Connecticut, Massachusetts, New Jersey, Maryland, and Rhode Island. Utah's population, however, is only 2.3 million people.

Origin of Utah's Name

Utah is named for the Ute nation of Native Americans. The word means "people of the mountains." The Ute called themselves Nuche.

Major Cities

Much of Utah's population is located in the Salt Lake valley, near the capital and largest city, Salt Lake City. The city is named for the Great Salt Lake, which is more than 72 miles wide and about six times saltier than the ocean. Salt Lake City is also home to the Mormon Church.

Provo, the third-largest city, is 45 miles south of Salt Lake City. It was named for a fur trapper who visited the area in the 1820s. Mormons settled Provo in 1849. Provo is the home of Brigham Young University, a Mormon university.

Saint George lies 260 miles south of Provo and is the largest city in southern Utah, with about 50,000 people.

*Mount Timpanogos, with an **elevation** of 11,750 feet, rises just north of Salt Lake City.*

Founded by Mormon settlers in 1861, the city grew from a small farming community to a major city. Today, area businesses include energy-related enterprises, manufacturing, and tourism.

Mormon settlers were discouraged from **prospecting** for minerals and coal by their leader and **prophet** Brigham Young. He wanted them to be farmers. However, in 1865, a Mormon discovered silver 58 miles south of Salt Lake City. This area became the Tintic Mining District, part of one of the richest mining regions in the West. The town of Eureka became home to four of the region's richest mines. It produced more than $500 million in silver, gold, and other minerals in its first 100 years. Today, Eureka has a population of only 766. Small mining operations continue, but most residents work for the government or in other industries.

Utah's Geography and Climate

Utah, the eleventh largest state in the country, is divided into three geographic regions: the Rocky Mountain region, the basin and range region, and the Colorado **Plateau.**

ROCKY MOUNTAINS

The Rocky Mountain region includes two groups of mountains, the Uinta range and the Wasatch range. The Uinta range reaches from Colorado in the east to the Salt Lake City area. It is the only Rocky Mountain range that runs east and west. Lakes and flat-bottomed canyons, formed by **glaciers,** are scattered between the mountains. Many peaks in the Uinta range are more than 13,000 feet above sea level. Kings Peak, at 13,528 feet above sea level, is the highest

Kings Peak is popular with hikers. An ascent generally takes two days.

Bonneville Salt Flats

The Bonneville Salt Flats International Speedway is a long, narrow strip of desert salt flat—the salty white bottom of an ancient lake, Lake Bonneville. Racers first brought their fastest cars to Bonneville in 1914. Many land speed records have been set there. A jet-powered car reached a speed of more than 600 miles per hour.

point in Utah. The Wasatch range stretches from north-central Utah northward into Idaho. These mountains reach heights of about 6,000 to 8,000 feet above sea level.

THE BASIN AND RANGE

One of the driest areas of the United States, the basin and ridge region spreads over the western part of the state. Small mountains and basins cover this area, and the Great Salt Lake is located in the northeastern corner. About 4,000 acres of hard, flat salt beds—the Bonneville Salt Flats—are located in the center of the nearby Great Salt Lake Desert.

THE COLORADO PLATEAU

The Colorado Plateau covers most of the southern and eastern areas of the state. Deep canyons and valleys are found here. The western part of the region includes high plateaus that tower more than 11,000 feet above sea level. Utah's southeastern corner meets the corners of Arizona, New Mexico, and Colorado. Referred to as Four Corners, this is the only place in the United States where four states meet.

Mountains occupy about a third of the land in Utah. The popular ski slopes can receive up to 400 inches of snow each winter.

UTAH'S CLIMATE AND PRECIPITATION

Utah's location helps explain its climate. The northern part of the state has cold, snowy winters, but temperatures rarely sink below 0°F. The southern part has warmer, dryer winter weather. In the summer, temperatures may reach 100°F, but the area's low humidity keeps it comfortable. Utah's climate is also affected by the difference in elevation between the desert and the mountains. Warm air naturally cools as it rises, so the temperatures in Utah's high mountains are much lower than the temperatures in the deserts.

Most of Utah is very dry. Deserts cover more than 30 percent of the state. Among the 50 states, only Nevada receives less **precipitation.** The driest areas are the Great Basin, the Uinta Basin, and the Colorado Plateau. These areas receive only five to ten inches of precipitation a year.

The Great Salt Lake

The Great Salt Lake is the largest body of water west of the Mississippi River. Streams and rivers flow into the Great Salt Lake, but none flow out. Thus, with the build up of minerals in the lake, it is the saltiest lake in the Western Hemisphere. The incoming water affects the lake's size. In 1962 it covered 969 square miles, but in 1983, after heavy rains, it grew to 2,300 square miles.

Average Annual Precipitation
Utah

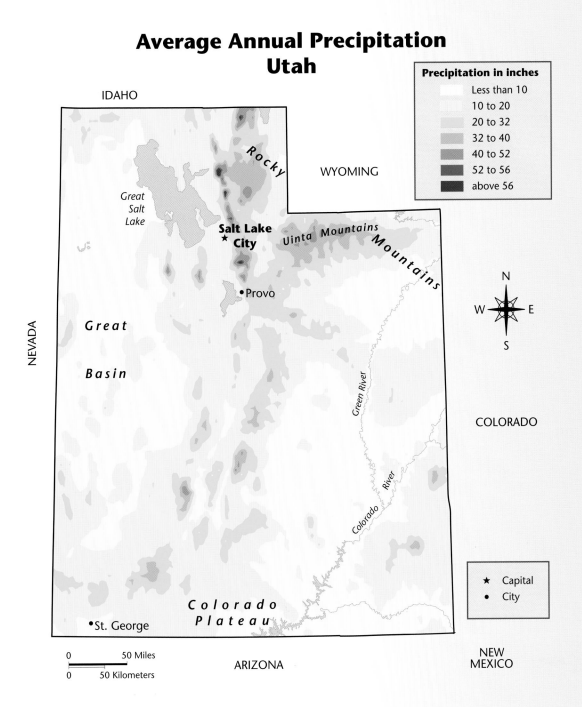

Precipitation in inches

	Less than 10
	10 to 20
	20 to 32
	32 to 40
	40 to 52
	52 to 56
	above 56

IDAHO

WYOMING

Rocky

Great Salt Lake

Salt Lake ★ City

Uinta Mountains

Mountains

•Provo

Great

Basin

N
W + E
S

Green River

COLORADO

Colorado River

★ Capital
• City

Colorado Plateau

•St. George

NEVADA

0	50 Miles
0	50 Kilometers

ARIZONA

NEW MEXICO

The highest peaks in Utah, mostly in the Rocky Mountain region, receive more than 500 inches of precipitation a year, most of which falls as snow. Skiers like Utah's dry and very light snow.

Famous Firsts

THE TRANSCONTINENTAL RAILROAD

On May 10, 1869, completion of the world's first **transcontinental** railroad was celebrated at Promontory Point, Utah. The Central Pacific and Union Pacific Railroads were joined, creating a railroad track that stretched across the United States from the East Coast to the West Coast. The transcontinental railroad opened up the West for more settlement.

David Hewes, a business leader, presented a golden spike when the transcontinental railroad was completed.

THE TRANSCONTINENTAL TELEGRAPH

The overland telegraph line was completed in Salt Lake City in 1861. The telegraph line connected Omaha, Nebraska, with San Francisco, California. Brigham Young helped with the project.

THE FIRST ARTIFICIAL HEART

Barney Clark, a retired dentist from Seattle, Washington, made history at the University of Utah Medical Center in Salt Lake City on December 1, 1982. He became the first person to receive an artificial heart. The plastic-and-aluminum heart kept him alive for 112 days after the surgery.

THE FIRST DEPARTMENT STORE

Utah is the home of the nation's first department store. Brigham Young, the second Mormon prophet, established

The ZCMI stores were in business for more than 100 years. In 1999, the Mormon Church sold ZCMI. The stores are now named Meier & Frank.

ZCMI, or the Zions Cooperative Mercantile Institution, in 1868. ZCMI sold everything the Mormon pioneers needed, including food, farm equipment, and cotton fabric.

THE DESERTED HIGHWAY

Interstate 70 enters Utah at its eastern edge and ends where it meets Interstate 15, near Cove Fort in southern Utah. This section of Interstate 70 is one of the most deserted stretches of highway in the United States. One can drive almost 100 miles without seeing a town or a gas station.

RAINBOW BRIDGE

Rainbow Bridge National Monument is a natural sandstone arch near Lake Powell. Spanning 270 feet and rising 290 feet high, it is the world's largest and most **symmetrical** natural rock bridge.

Visitors walk to Rainbow Bridge and gaze up at the natural wonder, which is located on the Navajo reservation.

MONUMENT VALLEY

Monument Valley is a land of red sandstone formations, many of which are 1,000 feet tall. The Paiute people, who hunted in the area, created myths about the sandstone figures. In one story, Totem Pole Rock is a god held up by lightning. In the light of the setting sun, this rock casts a 35-mile-long shadow.

Utah's State Symbols

UTAH STATE FLAG

Utah's first state flag was presented in 1896. In 1913, the state legislature adopted a new flag, which was almost identical to the original flag. This new flag, which Utah uses today, has a ring of gold around the state seal.

Utah's state flag is blue wi[th] a gold border. The state se[al] is in the center.

UTAH STATE SEAL

Harry Emmett Edwards designed Utah's state seal, which was adopted in 1896. A shield pierced by six arrows stands in the center of the seal. A bald eagle, the symbol of the United States, perches on top of the shield. This image stands for protection in peace and war. Beneath the eagle is a beehive, a symbol of **industry,** because bees are hardworking insects. The state flower, the sego lily, rests on either side of the hive, representing peace. Two U.S. flags symbolize Utah's support of the nation.

The state seal is printed on all official papers signed by Utah's governor.

STATE MOTTO: INDUSTRY

Utah's state motto is Industry. A picture of a beehive usually accompanies the motto. The early pioneers had few possessions and had to rely on their own industry, or hard work, to survive.

STATE NICKNAME: THE BEEHIVE STATE

Utah chose its nickname, the Beehive State, to represent the self-reliance of its people. Bees symbolize industry because they are hardworking insects.

STATE SONG: "UTAH . . . THIS IS THE PLACE"

A class of fourth-graders worked to change Utah's state song in 2003. The students said that the former state song, "Utah, We Love Thee," was not much fun to sing. The legislature voted to change the state song to "Utah . . . This is the Place," by Sam Francis and Gary

"Utah . . . This Is the Place"

Utah! People working together
Utah! What a great place to be.
Blessed from Heaven above.
It's the land that we love.
This is the place!

Utah! With its mountains and valleys.
Utah! With its canyons and streams.
You can go anywhere.
But there's none that compare.
This is the place!

It was Brigham Young who led the
 pioneers across the plains.
They suffered with the trials they had
 to face.
With faith they kept on going till they
 reached the Great Salt Lake
Here they heard the words . . .
 "THIS IS THE PLACE!"

School children across Utah voted to make the sego lily Utah's state flower.

Francis. The Francises wrote this song for the hundredth anniversary of Utah's statehood, in 1996. Evan Stephen wrote "Utah, We Love Thee," which is now the state anthem, for Utah's statehood celebration in 1896.

STATE FLOWER: SEGO LILY

The plain white blossom of the sego lily became the state flower in 1911. The root of the sego lily is like an onion and can be eaten. The Mormon pioneers, who first came to the state in 1847, depended on the sego root for food during their first winter in Utah.

Blue spruce needles are silvery blue. The tree can withstand extreme heat and cold.

STATE TREE: BLUE SPRUCE

The Utah legislature chose the blue spruce as Utah's state tree in 1933. The tree grows throughout Utah, especially in the Wasatch and Uinta mountains. Gardeners in Utah often use the blue spruce as a decorative tree in their yards.

STATE BIRD: CALIFORNIA GULL

The California gull was adopted as the state bird in 1955. An insect-eating bird, it lives on the west coast as well as in Utah. In 1848, the year after Mormon pioneers arrived in Utah, a **plague** of crickets attacked the fields and began to eat all of their crops. According to pioneer legends, flocks of California gulls swooped down and ate the crickets and thus saved the people from starvation.

STATE FISH: BONNEVILLE CUTTHROAT TROUT

Named the state fish in 1997, the Bonneville cutthroat trout is native to Utah. It was an important source of food for Native Americans and Mormon pioneers.

The cutthroat trout gets its name from the red or orange stripe on its throat that looks like a cut.

STATE GRASS: INDIAN RICE GRASS

Indian rice grass, a native desert grass, was chosen as the state grass in 1990. This grass grows as high as two feet tall, and its seeds are about half the size of a grain of rice. Native Americans gathered the seeds for food.

Ranchers value Indian rice grass as winter feed for their animals.

Elk herds are plentiful on most mountain ranges in Utah.

STATE MAMMAL: ROCKY MOUNTAIN ELK

Named the state mammal in 1971, the Rocky Mountain elk spends summers in the mountains and winters in the state's lower valleys. Males grow to be about 60 inches tall and weigh more than 700 pounds. Females are smaller than males and do not have antlers.

*The Japanese sent cherry trees to Utah after **World War II** (1941–1945). The cherry tree is a sign of friendship.*

STATE FRUIT: CHERRY

A second-grade class from Millville named the cherry as the state fruit in 1997. The class researched the peach, apple, and cherry. They discovered that the cherry was more important to Utah's economy than the other two fruits. Utah is the second-largest tart cherry producer in the country and the fifth-largest sweet cherry producer. No other state ranks in the top five in both categories.

STATE FOSSIL: ALLOSAURUS

Dinosaur bones are plentiful in Utah. The skeleton of a sixteen-foot-tall, four-ton, meat-eating allosaurus is Utah's state fossil. It was chosen in 1988. More than 60 allosaurus skeletons have been found in one **quarry** in Utah.

STATE INSECT: HONEYBEE

A fifth-grade class in Salt Lake County worked for the honeybee to be named state insect in 1983. The hardworking bee is a symbol of industry. The word Deseret, the

Honeybees build nests, or combs of wax, which is released by glands in their stomachs.

name given to Utah by the **Mormon** pioneers, means "honeybee" in the *Book of Mormon,* the Mormon religious book.

STATE GEM: TOPAZ

In 1969, Utah named the topaz as the state **gem.** A hard gem, topaz is mined in Beaver, Juab, and Tooele counties. Sometimes topaz is colorless, but it is usually pale blue, yellow, or pink.

STATE MINERAL: COPPER

Named the state mineral in 1994, most of the copper mined in Utah comes from the Kennecott Bingham Canyon Mine west of the Salt Lake valley. This mine, the world's largest open-pit copper mine, is nearly a mile deep. It produces about 260,000 tons of refined copper each year.

The ancient Greeks believed that people who wore topaz around their neck could grow stronger and become invisible in an emergency.

STATE ROCK: COAL

In 1991, Representative Mike Dmitrich of Price, in Carbon County, proposed that coal be named the state rock. Coal is one of the most important rocks in Utah's **economy.** It is found in 17 of the state's 29 counties. More than half of Utah's electricity is created by coal-burning power plants.

Utah produces about 24 million tons of coal each year.

Utah's History and People

Today, about 89 percent of Utah's citizens have European **ancestors.** However, the first people who lived in the region were Native Americans. Later, Spanish, French, and American explorers traveled to the area. Mormon pioneers and eastern European laborers followed.

EARLIEST NATIVE PEOPLE

Native Americans lived in Utah for at least 10,000 years before European settlers arrived. The Anasazi and Fremont cultures are two of the prehistoric Native American groups that once lived in Utah. These cultures began almost 2,000 years ago. By about 1,000 years ago, these cultures had weakened, and new tribes moved into the area. The Ute came to the area about 700 years ago and still live in Utah.

Many Native Americans were **nomadic,** but the Anasazi were farmers. They grew squash, beans, and corn. They also built stone villages in the deserts of southern Utah. One example, Hovenweep National Monument, includes five prehistoric Anasazi villages spread over twenty miles of canyons and the tops of **mesas.** These villages, called **cliff dwellings,** were built high on the cliff wall and so protected the Anasazi from the weather and from attack by other tribes.

THE UTE

The Anasazi disappeared from Utah by about 1300. They are thought to have moved south to present-day

The Anasazi made buildings, such as this one, long before the arrival of Columbus, more than 1,000 years ago.

Arizona and New Mexico. Some **archaeologists** believe the Anasazi left because of drought, overused soil, and cooler weather. Others believe that new tribes invaded the area and forced the Anasazi to leave. The tribes that followed the Anasazi are the Ute, Paiute, and Navajo.

The Ute were made up of several nomadic tribes. The men hunted deer and other animals. The women gathered grass, seeds, and roots for food and to make clothing.

EARLY EXPLORERS

Father Anastasio Domínguez and Father Silvestre Velez de Escalante, two Spanish priests, were the among the first Europeans to explore Utah. These **missionaries** wanted the Native Americans to become Christians.

The missionaries left Santa Fe, New Mexico, as part of an **expedition,** on July 29, 1776. They hoped to find a northern route from New Mexico to Monterey, California. They decided on a route through the land of the Ute, who were known to be friendly.

After three months of travel, the weather turned cold and forced the party to return to New Mexico before they found a route to California. They arrived in Santa Fe in January 1777, after traveling more than 1,700 miles.

Priests were the among the first Europeans to explore what is today Utah. They kept journals that included maps and that described the land, plants, animals, and people of Utah. Their journal and maps helped open the Old Spanish Trail between New Mexico and California 40 years later. John C. Frémont, an American general, used this information during his expedition to the region in 1843 and 1844.

THE MORMON PIONEERS

In 1847, members of the Church of Jesus Christ of Latter-day Saints, also called the Mormon Church, arrived in Utah. The **Mormons** were the first European American settlers in Utah.

The Mormon leader Brigham Young brought the Mormons to the Salt Lake valley in 1847 to escape religious **persecution** in Illinois.

The first Mormon settlement, called Desert, was established in Salt Lake City. The Mormon Church gave every Mormon family enough land for a house, an orchard, and a garden. The church printed money for its members.

These coins and paper money were used by Mormon pioneers.

Ensign Peak

On July 26, 1847, Brigham Young and several others climbed a stone-capped peak so they could see the entire Salt Lake valley. Young named the peak Ensign Peak, because he believed it was a sign of prosperity and peace for his people. He said he had a vision of this peak while he was still in Illinois and that Joseph Smith, the founder of the Mormon Church, told him to build a city at the foot of this mountain.

The early Mormon farmers faced new problems. Little rain fell in the hot, dusty summer, and the soil was hard and dry. Plants did not grow well. The Mormons dug **irrigation** canals that carried water from the rivers into the fields. By 1865, the settlers had dug more than 1,000 miles of canals to water their crops.

THE UTAH WAR

In the fall of 1857, President James Buchanan sent U.S. troops to Utah to force Brigham Young to resign as governor because Young allowed his followers to practice polygamy.

Cold weather stopped the troops before they reached the Salt Lake valley. The Mormons burned the army's trains and scared off their animals. Even though neither side actually fought and nobody was killed, this event became known as the Utah War. By the spring of 1858, the Utah War was over. Alfred Cumming became the new governor of Utah. After a few days, the Mormons came back to their homes in the city.

The Coming of the Railroads

The railroad came to the West in 1869. It brought people of all religions and **cultures** to work and live in Utah.

The railroad helped Utah's mining industry become efficient. Miners could now ship coal, gold, iron ore, and copper ore by rail. Railroads also served **agriculture.** Trains carried Utah dairy products, wheat, sugar beets, and fruits and vegetables to markets outside the state.

Statehood

Although Utah became a territory in 1850, it did not become a state for another 46 years. The U.S. government refused to admit Utah to the Union because it did not want Americans to practice polygamy. In 1896, the Mormon Church agreed to stop teaching polygamy. Finally, on January 4, 1896, Utah became the forty-fifth state.

Topaz Relocation Center

After the United States entered **World War II** in 1941, the U.S. government forced Japanese Americans to move out of their homes. Topaz Relocation Center opened in the western Utah desert in 1942. Eight thousand Japanese Americans lived in this one-square-mile camp. In 1976, the Japanese-American Citizens League built a monument at the site of the camp. In 1988, President Ronald Reagan apologized to all the people who had lived in the camps.

FAMOUS PEOPLE

Brigham Young (1801–1877), religious leader, territorial governor. Brigham Young was born in Wittingham, Vermont. He became the second president of the Mormon Church. He brought the first European American settlers to Utah in 1847.

Martha Hughes Cannon (1857–1932), state senator. Martha Hughes Cannon graduated from medical school in 1882 and became a physician. In 1896, she ran for a seat in the Utah Senate. Her husband was also one of the candidates running for a seat, but she won. She became the first female state senator in the United States.

Heber Manning Wells (1859–1938), politician. Heber Manning Wells served as Utah's first state governor from 1896 to 1905. In 1897, he helped write the state's first laws dealing with irrigation and water rights.

Brigham Young designed the original plan for Salt Lake City, established stores, built irrigation systems, and helped the Mormon pioneers establish towns throughout the Utah territory.

Reed Smoot (1862–1941) U.S. senator. Born in Salt Lake City, Reed Smoot was the first Mormon elected to the U.S. Senate. After his election, in 1902, the Senate debated whether Smoot should be allowed to serve as senator because he was a Mormon. The Senate finally decided that Mormons have the right to hold political office.

Butch Cassidy (1867–unknown), outlaw. Born Robert Leroy Parker in Beaver, Butch Cassidy was an infamous outlaw, known for cattle rustling, horse theft, and train robbery. Cassidy and his gang, the Wild Bunch, hid in the southeastern Utah desert near Green River. No one knows for certain what happened to Cassidy.

Philo Farnsworth attended Brigham Young University but left school after only two years.

J. Willard Marriott (1900–1985), restaurant and hotel-chain founder J. Willard Marriott was born near Ogden. Marriott's first restaurant was a Washington, D.C., drive-in called the Hot Shoppe. The Marriott Corporation expanded and opened its first hotels in 1957.

Philo P. Farnsworth (1906–1971), inventor. Born near Beaver City, Philo P. Farnsworth first had the idea for television at age fourteen. He transmitted the first, rough, television picture in 1927. In 1928, the first commercial television was produced.

Roseanne Barr (1952–), comedian and actress. Roseanne Barr was born in Salt Lake City, where she grew up both Jewish and Mormon. Her hit television series, *Roseanne*, ran for nine years during the 1980s and 1990s.

Donny Osmond, Marie Osmond (1957– ; 1959–) entertainers. The Osmonds were born in Provo. Marie was three years old and Donny was five when they started singing on national television. Donny and Marie have hosted television programs and acted in professional theater.

Donny and Marie Osmond were major pop music stars in the 1970s.

Steve Young (1961–), football player. A great-great grandson of Brigham Young, Steve Young was born in Salt Lake City. As a quarterback, Young helped the San Francisco 49ers win three Super Bowl championships.

Temple Square

Temple Square in Salt Lake City is one of the most famous **landmarks** in Utah. It is the site of the Salt Lake City Temple, the main temple of the Mormon Church. In the temple, believers hold baptism and **eternal** marriage ceremonies. A fifteen-foot-high wall surrounds the temple and nearby church buildings. Across the street to the east is Brigham Young's original house.

BUILDING THE TEMPLE

The design for the Salt Lake City Temple came to Brigham Young in a vision. The Mormons began building the temple in 1853, and it took 40 years to complete. They used blocks of **granite,** quarried in a canyon twenty miles from the city. Workers cut the stone by hand and hauled it by ox-pulled carts. Later, the workers sent the stone by rail. The temple is built of more than 7,000 tons of stone.

The Salt Lake City Temple is designed with six large towers, each one crowned with **spires.** The temple has many

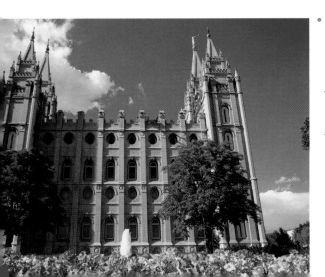

Sandstone for the Temple's 46 supporting pillars was shipped from Red Butte Canyon, east of Salt Lake City. Nearly two million feet of lumber was hauled from the Wasatch Mountains to complete the construction.

The Mormon Tabernacle Choir's Organ

The Mormon Tabernacle's organ is famous around the world. A huge musical instrument, it includes about 12,000 pipes, 5 keyboards, and 1 pedal keyboard.

small rooms where the faithful perform religious ceremonies and receive religious training. Although many of the buildings and visitor centers on Temple Square are open to the public, the temple itself is open only to members of the Mormon Church who have special permission.

THE TEMPLE TODAY

Mormon temples have been built over the world, but the Salt Lake City Temple is the center of the Mormon Church. Salt Lake City is where Brigham Young and his followers chose to create their "heavenly kingdom on Earth."

The Salt Lake City Temple attracts visitors from all over the world. Many are faithful Mormons who believe that Temple Square is a sacred place. Some are simply curious, while others come to experience history.

THE MORMON TABERNACLE CHOIR

The Mormon Tabernacle Choir is one of the most famous vocal groups in the world. The choir, numbering 360 people, sings for religious services and appears on television and radio. The choir first started singing on the radio in 1929.

Pioneers worked for four years to build the famous tabernacle where the Mormon Tabernacle Choir sings.

Utah's State Government

Utah is governed from Salt Lake City, the capital, under a constitution, a plan of government approved by the state's people.

Utah's constitution went into effect at statehood in 1896. It promises many of the same freedoms guaranteed by the U.S. Constitution, including freedom of religion, speech, and the press. Like the **federal government** in Washington, D.C., Utah's government is made up of three branches—legislative, executive, and judicial.

THE LEGISLATIVE BRANCH

Utah's **legislature** makes the state's laws. It consists of two houses—the senate, whose 29 members are elected to four-year terms, and the house of representatives,

Utah's capitol was built to look like the U.S. Capitol.

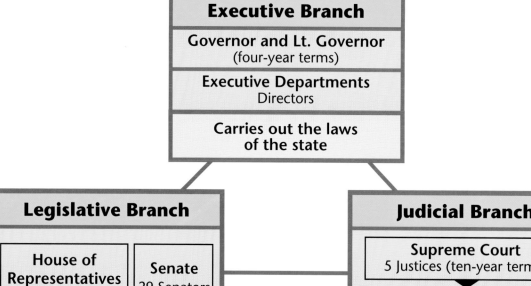

Executive Branch
Governor and Lt. Governor (four-year terms)
Executive Departments Directors
Carries out the laws of the state

Legislative Branch
House of Representatives 75 Representatives (two-year terms) / **Senate** 29 Senators (four-year terms)
Makes laws for the state

Judicial Branch
Supreme Court 5 Justices (ten-year terms)
Court of Appeals 7 Judges (six-year terms)
District Courts
Explains laws

whose 75 members are elected to two-year terms. In 2003, Utah's legislature **repealed** the state's term-limit laws.

Utah's legislators are citizen-legislators, that is, most of them have other, full-time jobs. Legislators live throughout Utah and travel to the capital for legislative sessions, which last 45 days.

A bill, or proposed law, may start in either house of the legislature. After a bill has been approved by a majority (more than half) of the members of both houses, it is sent to the governor to be signed into law. If the governor vetoes (rejects) the bill, it becomes law only if a majority of the legislature votes to override the veto.

Olene Walker is Utah's first female governor—the highest-ranking female officeholder in state history.

THE EXECUTIVE BRANCH

The executive branch enforces the state's laws and runs the state from day to day. The governor, who is elected to a four-year term, is the head of this branch. He is assisted by the lieutenant governor.

Other elected officials in the executive branch include the secretary of state, the attorney general, and the treasurer.

THE JUDICIAL BRANCH

The district courts are the main trial courts in the state. Seventy district judges serve the state's eight judicial districts. District courts have the power to try all **civil cases** and **criminal cases,** including murders, drug offenses, and robberies. The juvenile court is similar to a district court but only hears cases dealing with people under age eighteen who violate the law. The juvenile court can also place children in foster homes or determine child custody in a divorce case.

The Utah Supreme Court meets at the Matheson Courthouse in Salt Lake City.

The Utah court of appeals, created in 1987, hears all appeals from the juvenile and district courts. Its seven judges serve six-year renewable terms. A presiding judge is elected by majority vote to serve for two years. The court of appeals usually sits in Salt Lake City, but the court also travels several times each year holding court in different parts of the state.

The Utah Supreme Court is the highest court in the state. The court's five justices serve ten-year renewable terms. The justices elect a chief justice by majority vote to serve for four years and an associate chief justice to serve for two years.

Utah's Culture

People of many backgrounds give Utah its unique culture. Members of the Mormon Church and Native Americans make up a large part of the population. More than 40 ethnic groups live in Utah.

FESTIVALS

Immigrants have played an important role in Utah's history, and Utahns today celebrate their cultures and contributions. For example, the southeastern town of Price has International Days, and the northern town of Midway has Swiss Days.

The Living Traditions Festival is a popular yearly event that brings together the many cultures within the state. During this May festival, held in Salt Lake City, performing artists show off their cultural heritage with traditional costumes and dances and the sound of bagpipes, Caribbean dance music, Japanese drumming, and American rhythm and blues. Ethnic foods include Greek gyros, Chinese sesame chicken, and Peruvian tamales. **Artisans** demonstrate how to make a variety of traditional items, including lace, saddles, and Navaho rugs.

The weekend festival features traditional arts, entertainment, crafts and food from more than 40 ethnic communities.

Many Basque people, a group whose homeland is in northeastern Spain and southeastern France, moved to Utah in the late 1800s. The Basques worked as shepherds on the ranches and in the copper mines. Today, they preserve their culture through traditional Basque dances, music, language, games, and Roman Catholic religious ceremonies. The Utah'ko Triskalariak Basque Dancers, a traditional dance troupe, performs throughout the western United States.

THE DAYS OF '47

Mormon history is an important part of Utah's culture. Utahns celebrate the first Mormon settlers' arrival into the Salt Lake Valley with the Days of '47 festival. Mormons first arrived on July 24, 1847, and today Utahns hold a celebration every July 24.

The women in this photograph are dressed like the Mormon pioneers of 1847.

During the Days of '47, people watch a parade of floats and marching bands in downtown Salt Lake City. The city also has an all-horse parade, one of the largest horse parades in the country with more than 500 kinds of horses.

Runners compete in a ten-kilometer race. The racecourse follows the last part of the historic Mormon Trail, the route Mormon settlers used to enter the valley. Athletes from all over the world come to compete in this race.

Another important Days of '47 activity is the rodeo. In the past, cowboys had informal rodeos at the close of long cattle drives. Today, cowhands compete in official rodeos. The Days of '47 Rodeo is one of the few indoor rodeos in the country.

Utah's Food

BEEF

Like many western states, cattle ranches are found throughout Utah. Thus, beef is a favorite dish of many of the state's people. One meal some Utahns enjoy is Utah steak and beans, a skillet dish made with steak, beans, onions, honey, and mustard.

Chocolate Rice Custard Freeze

Utahns love all types of dessert. One favorite is Chocolate Rice Custard Freeze.
Be sure to have an adult help you with the recipe.

1-1/2 cups cooked rice

1 cup sugar

4 4-ounce squares unsweetened
    chocolate, melted

1/8 teaspoon salt

3 cups milk   2 cups heavy cream

2 eggs, beaten   1 tablespoon vanilla extract

Combine rice, sugar, chocolate, salt, milk, and eggs in large saucepan. Cook over low heat until mixture just begins to bubble, stirring constantly; cool. Add cream and vanilla. Prepare ice cream freezer according to manufacturer's directions. Pour mixture into freezer can and freeze as directed. Makes eight servings.

In 1845 the inventor Peter Cooper obtained the first patent for a gelatin dessert. In 1895 Pearl Wait, a cough syrup manufacturer, bought the patent from Cooper and turned the dessert into a packaged product. His wife, May Wait, renamed the dessert "Jell-O."

JELL-O: UTAH'S FAVORITE SNACK FOOD

Utahns love Jell-O gelatin. People in Salt Lake City eat twice as much of the wiggly food as people in other cities of the United States. Utah has an official Jell-O week, and a bowl of Jell-O is pictured on an official Utah Olympic collector's pin. In 2001, Utah's legislators named Jell-O the official state snack food after 15,000 Utahns urged them to do so.

TRADITIONAL BASQUE DISHES

The Basque tradition of hearty meals continues in Utah today. Generous meals often include beef and lamb steaks, soup, salad, beans, spaghetti, and bread. Another Basque specialty is chorizo, a spicy sausage. Garlic is a favorite herb in Basque cooking.

Utah's Folklore and Legends

Legends and folklore are stories that are not totally true but are often based on bits of truth. These stories help people understand things that are not easily explained. They also teach lessons to younger generations. All peoples have passed down stories as part of their culture.

THE BEAR LAKE MONSTER

One famous Utah legend begins in northern Utah's cold Bear Lake when Native Americans first saw a strange creature swimming in the lake. It looked like a snake or dragon, and according to legend, it ate people.

An 1868 article in the *Deseret News* described this "monster" as brown, between 40 and 200 feet long, with a head like a walrus or an alligator. It swam about 60 miles per hour and had many legs. No one had ever seen the monster on land.

In 1871, a fisher near the town of Fish Haven claimed he trapped the Bear Lake monster. The creature he caught was about 20 feet long and had a large mouth, legs, and a tail. Some people say his catch was a fake—a large codfish with eight chicken legs attached to its body.

THE BUFFALO HUNTING PORCUPINE

The Ute people tell the legend of Buffalo Hunting Porcupine.

Porcupine asks Buffalo to carry him across the river inside his belly. In this way, Porcupine can stay dry. Buffalo agrees, and after they have crossed the river, Buffalo asks Porcupine to crawl out of his belly. Instead, Porcupine sticks Buffalo's heart with his quills and kills him.

This Ute legend teaches children about trusting others. Some people, like Buffalo, learn too late. Others, like Porcupine, do not keep their word and are not to be trusted.

Utah's Sports Teams

Ski-jumping, luge, snowboarding, skiing, speed-skating, and ice-skating competitions are popular Utah winter sports. In 2002, Salt Lake City hosted the Winter Olympic Games.

Utah is home to several college athletic teams and a professional sports team. The Utah Jazz is a National Basketball Association (NBA) pro basketball team.

THE JAZZ

Utah is not famous for jazz music, so where did the NBA basketball team the Utah Jazz get its name? The Jazz basketball team originated in Louisiana in 1974. The team was named for the jazz music that is important in that state. Its colors—purple, green, and gold—are the colors of Louisiana's annual Mardi Gras celebration. The team moved to Utah in 1979 and kept its name.

The Utah Jazz is one of the leading basketball teams in the NBA. The Jazz play in the Delta Center in Salt Lake City. Karl Malone and John Stockton are two of the

The Utah Jazz started out as the New Orleans Jazz in 1974 before moving to Salt Lake City in 1979.

team's best-known former players. Stockton and Malone played seventeen straight seasons together. The Jazz made it to the NBA finals in 1997 and 1998 and have been in the playoffs for nineteen straight years.

UNIVERSITY SPORTS

Brigham Young University (BYU) in Provo has one of the best women's cross-country teams in the United States. BYU's team has won four national championships since the program started in 1981. The team won 83 races and placed first in 19 of the last 20 conference championships.

The women's gymnastics team at the University of Utah is another winning team. They have won 768 meets against other collegiate teams and 10 national championships in the last 27 years. Between 1981 and 1986, the gymnasts won the national championship every year. More than 10,000 fans attend each meet.

The University of Utah men's and women's cross-country and downhill ski teams have won ten national championship titles since 1978. Twenty-seven Utah skiers have become U.S. Olympic athletes. Three of them competed in the Olympics for other countries. Torin Koos and Kristina Joder competed in the Olympics in Salt Lake City in 2002.

The University of Utah ski team is ranked #1 in the United States.

Utah's Businesses and Products

Ranching, farming, and mining are a part of daily life for many Utahns in small towns. Many people in Utah's cities work for the government and the universities.

AGRICULTURE

Agriculture is an important part of Utah's economy. More than 100,000 Utahns work in agriculture. About 15,000 farms are spread across the state, totaling nearly 11.6 million acres. Utah produces crops and livestock worth nearly $1 billion annually. Utah ranks second in the nation in the production of tart cherries, ninth in spring wheat, and ninth in onions. Utah farmers also produce sheep, turkeys, hogs, chickens, milk, hay, and other grains.

CATTLE RANCHING

Beef is Utah's top product. Because of the state's many open spaces and its small population, even today cattle graze on public land. Cattle ranching began in the 1840s, when the Mormon pioneers in Utah raised cattle on their land. In time, huge cattle companies came to the state. Today, there are nearly 1 million head of cattle in Utah.

Cattle herding is one of the last links between the old west and the new.

The giant electric shovels that work the Kennecott Bingham mine can scoop up about 98 tons of rock and minerals at one time—about the weight of 50 cars.

MINING

Mining has been part of Utah's economy since the 1850s. Gold, silver, copper, magnesium, uranium, coal, and salt are all mined in Utah. Oil, too, is an important resource in the state. Utah's copper and gold are used in Asia to make computer chips. Utah's coal is in demand because it has a low amount of sulfur. When low-sulfur coal is burned, it causes less air pollution than high-sulfur coal.

Kennecott Bingham Canyon Mine

Kennecott Bingham Canyon Mine is the largest and oldest open-pit copper mine in the world. The mine's wealth was discovered by U.S. soldiers in 1863. Since then, the mine has produced more than sixteen million tons of copper, as well as some gold and silver. The mine is two and one half miles wide and three-quarters of a mile deep.

Attractions and Landmarks

The vast stretches of Utah's deserts and the state's grand mountain ranges offer unmatched beauty for Utahns and visitors alike. Utah's historical landmarks are unlike those of any other state.

NATIONAL PARKS

Utah is home to five national parks—Arches, Canyonlands, Bryce Canyon, Capitol Reef, and Zion. Each one of Utah's national parks is unique. Arches is known for its many red sandstone arches, while Canyonlands is a maze of canyons and rivers. In Bryce Canyon, there are limestone pillars hundreds of feet high. Capitol Reef is known for the Waterpocket Fold, where forces within the earth folded and pushed up the land. Zion Canyon, more than 2,400 feet deep, cuts through Zion National Park. All of Utah's national parks are in the Colorado Plateau region, in the southern part of the state.

Zion National Park is rated one of the top national parks.

DANGER CAVE

Danger Cave provides clues about Utah's ancient history. **Archaeologists** have discovered thousands of Native American **artifacts** in this western Utah cave. The oldest artifacts, which are about 10,000 years old, include arrow shafts, knives, drills, baskets, and moccasins. Danger Cave was given its name when a huge piece of the ceiling fell down in the 1950s.

FORT DOUGLAS

Established on October 26, 1862, Fort Douglas was home to U.S. Army troops until October 26, 1991, when most

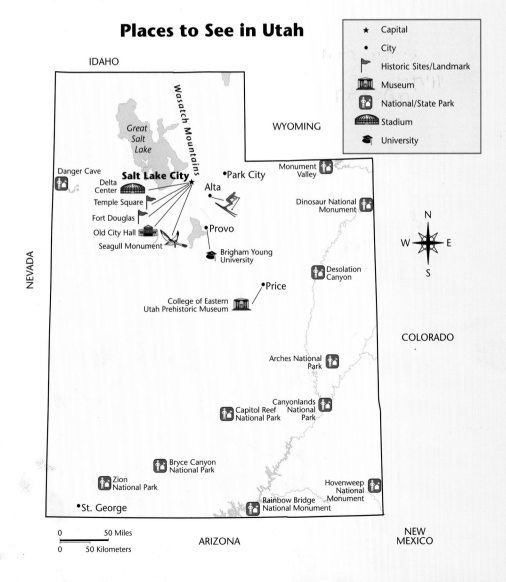

Places to See in Utah

Capital
City
Historic Sites/Landmark
Museum
National/State Park
Stadium
University

IDAHO

WYOMING

Great
Salt
Lake

Wasatch Mountains

Danger Cave

Salt Lake City

Delta
Center

Temple Square

Fort Douglas

Old City Hall

Seagull Monument

Park City

Alta

Provo

Brigham Young
University

Monument
Valley

Dinosaur National
Monument

Desolation
Canyon

Price

College of Eastern
Utah Prehistoric Museum

NEVADA

N
W   E
S

COLORADO

Arches National
Park

Canyonlands
National
Park

Capitol Reef
National Park

Bryce Canyon
National Park

Zion
National Park

St. George

Hovenweep
National
Monument

Rainbow Bridge
National Monument

0   50 Miles
0   50 Kilometers

ARIZONA

NEW
MEXICO

Desolation Canyon

The explorer John Wesley Powell named Desolation Canyon when he began to chart the area in 1869. Today, Desolation Canyon is a favorite vacation stop. It offers visitors breathtaking scenery, including redrock canyon walls, towering sandstone cliffs, and orange-red sunsets. Rafting trips through the canyon section last between four and six days. In addition to the scenery, visitors can see Native American ruins and historical rock art sites. Among the wild animals in the canyon are eagles, bears, elk, deer, and beavers.

of the fort was turned over to the University of Utah. Parts of the fort still serve the U.S. military and the Utah National Guard.

In the 1860s, the fort's troops guarded the overland mail route between the eastern states and California. The importance of the fort grew as a military and trading center as settlers moved westward. By about 1900, the fort became an important training base for troops. By 1940, Fort Douglas grew to include three separate bases—the fort, the Salt Lake airbase, and the Wendover Bombing and Gunnery Range.

The historic area of Fort Douglas was designated a National Historic Landmark in 1970. Today, tourists can see museum exhibits, visit restored military buildings, and learn about life at the fort. During the 2002 Salt Lake City winter games, the Fort Douglas barracks housed Olympic athletes. These buildings are now dormitories for university students.

OLD CITY HALL

Built in 1866, Salt Lake City's first city hall was made of red sandstone. The Utah territorial legislature met here and passed laws that established free public schools, set up the University of Utah, and granted women the right to vote. From its tower, a 1,700-pound bell sounded fire alarms. In 1961, the old city hall building was taken down, rebuilt, and restored on the grounds of the Utah state capitol. Visitors can see original furniture and other items dating back to the 1860's.

DINOSAUR NATIONAL MONUMENT

Created in 1915, seven years after the first fossilized dinosaur bones were discovered there, Dinosaur National Monument now stretches across 200,000 acres. The

Buried by sand and mud, the preserved fossils of dinosaurs, alligators, and frogs show us the animals that once lived in Utah.

monument includes two areas. The smaller part, called the quarry area, contains a quarry with about 1,600 exposed bones from eleven different types of dinosaurs. The rock surrounding the bones has been carefully scraped away so that visitors can easily see them, which include nearly full dinosaur skeletons. Canyon country is the larger area of the park. Its deep canyons were carved by the Green and Yampa rivers thousands of years ago.

PARK CITY

In 1869, silver ore was discovered in Park City, a town 27 miles northeast of Salt Lake City. Hundreds of miners from all over the world came to Park City between 1870 and 1900. In the late twentieth century, Park City became a town of ski resorts.

The powder ski conditions produced in this range are world renowned.

SKI RESORTS

Some of the oldest ski resorts in the United States are in Utah's Wasatch Mountains. Alta began as a mining town but turned into a ski resort in the 1930s. In 1939, a chairlift began hauling people to the tops of Alta's slopes for 25 cents a ride or $1.50 for a full day. Today, ski resorts such as Snowbird, Solitude, and Deer Valley dot Utah's mountains.

Map of Utah

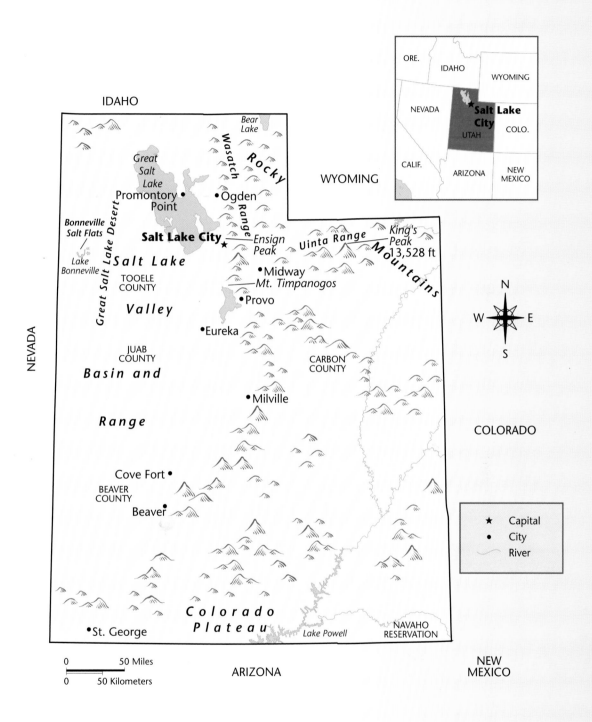

IDAHO

Bear Lake

Great Salt Lake

Promontory Point

Bonneville Salt Flats

Lake Bonneville

Great Salt Lake Desert

Wasatch Range

Rocky

•Ogden

Salt Lake City★

Ensign Peak

Uinta Range

King's Peak 13,528 ft

Mountains

WYOMING

Salt Lake

TOOELE COUNTY

Valley

•Midway

Mt. Timpanogos

•Provo

•Eureka

JUAB COUNTY

Basin and

Range

•Milville

CARBON COUNTY

COLORADO

Cove Fort •

BEAVER COUNTY

Beaver•

Colorado

Plateau

•St. George

Lake Powell

NAVAHO RESERVATION

ORE.

IDAHO

WYOMING

NEVADA

★**Salt Lake City**

UTAH

COLO.

CALIF.

ARIZONA

NEW MEXICO

NEVADA

N

W E

S

★	Capital
•	City
⌇	River

| 0 | 50 Miles |
| 0 | 50 Kilometers |

ARIZONA

NEW MEXICO

Glossary

agriculture having to do with farming

archaeologists social scientists who study the cultural remains of earlier people

ancestors persons from whom one is descended

artifacts items such as pottery, arrowheads, and tools left by earlier cultures

artisans artists and craftspeople

civil cases court actions between individuals having to do with property rights and other noncriminal matters

cliff dwellings homes made on the side of a cliff or mountain, often for protection from enemies

criminal cases court actions dealing with violations of the criminal law

culture the way of life, customs, and traditions of a group of people

economy a system that carefully manages resources, such as money, material, or labor

elevation the distance above sea level

eternal something that lasts forever

expedition a journey made in order to explore an area

federal government the national government

gem a precious stone, often used in jewelry

glaciers thick, slow-moving sheets of ice that wear away the soil as they move

granite a type of very hard, strong stone used in building

immigrants people who leave one country and settle in another one

industry the quality of being hardworking

irrigation the process by which water is supplied to crops by artificial means

landmarks buildings or natural objects that are given special importance

legislature group of elected officials who make laws

mesas large, flat areas on top of hills and mountains

missionaries people who teach religion in a foreign land

Mormons members of the Church of Jesus Christ of Latter-day Saints, founded by Joseph Smith

nomadic referring to animals or people who move from place to place to find food or shelter

ore minerals mixed with dirt and rocks

persecution harming people guilty of no crime, for example, their beliefs or lifestyle

plague a serious disaster, such as the sudden appearance of destructive insects or disease

plateau a broad, level, flat, elevated area of land; a tableland

precipitation a form of water, such as rain, snow, or sleet, that condenses from the atmosphere and falls to the surface of the earth

prophet a person who speaks words inspired by God and so expresses God's message to other people

prospecting searching for mineral deposits, such as gold, silver, or copper

quarry an open pit or hole from which rock or stone is mined, sometimes revealing buried fossils

repealed no longer enforced; said, for example, of a law or rule

spires the pointed tops of pillars; a spire is similar to a steeple

symmetrical one side of an object being a mirror image of the other

transcontinental stretching across a continent

World War II the war (1939–1945) between the Allies (Great Britain, France, Russia, the United States) and the Axis (Germany, Italy, Japan)

More Books to Read

Deady, Kathleen. *Utah.* Mankato, MN: Capstone Press, 2003.

Ferguson, Alane and Gloria Skurzynski. *Ghost Horses (Mysteries in Our National Parks).* Washington, D.C.: National Geographic, 2000.

Kent, Deborah. *Utah (America the Beautiful).* Minneapolis, MN: Children's Press, 2000.

Litchman, Kristin Embry. *All Is Well.* New York: Delacorte Press, 1998.

London, Jonathon. *White Water.* New York: Viking Children's Books, 2001.

Petersen, David. *Arches National Park (A True Book).* Danbury, Conn.: Children's Press, 1999.

Index

About the Authors

Bianca Dumas is the author of five books for children and young adults. She has also written many magazine articles. Ms. Dumas lives in Helper, Utah.

D. J. Ross is a writer and educator with more than 25 years of experience in education. He has lived throughout the United States but now lives in the Midwest with his three basset hounds.